WORLD OF
REPTILES

GILA MONSTERS

by Sophie Lockwood

Content Adviser: Harold K. Voris, PhD, Curator and Head,
Amphibians and Reptiles, Department of Zoology,
The Field Museum, Chicago, Illinois

THE CHILD'S WORLD®, CHANHASSEN, MINNESOTA

GILA MONSTERS

Published in the United States of America by The Child's World®
PO Box 326 • Chanhassen, MN 55317-0326 • 800-599-READ • www.childsworld.com

Acknowledgements:

The Child's World®: Mary Berendes, Publishing Director

Editorial Directions, Inc.: E. Russell Primm, Editorial Director; Pam Rosenberg, Editor; Judith Shiffer, Assistant Editor; Caroline Wood and Rory Mabin, Editorial Assistants; Susan Hindman, Copy Editor; Emily Dolbear and Sarah E. De Capua, Proofreaders; Elizabeth Nellums, Olivia Nellums, and Daisy Porter, Fact Checkers; Tim Griffin/ IndexServ, Indexer; Cian Loughlin O'Day, Photo Researcher, Linda S. Koutris, Photo Editor

The Design Lab: Kathleen Petelinsek, Art Director, Cartographer; Julia Goozen, Page Production Artist

Photos:

Cover/ 2-3: Tim Flach / Stone / Getty Images; frontispiece / 4: Steve Kaufman / Corbis.

Interior: amy Images: 5-top left and 8 (Andrew Harrington), 34 (David R. Frazier Photolibrary Inc.); Animals Animals / Earth Scenes: 16 (Zigmund Leszczynski), 24 (McDonald Wildlife Photography); Corbis: 5-bottom right and 27 (Lindsay Hebberd), 36 (Steve Kaufman); Getty Images: 5-top right and 19 (Tim Flach / Stone), 5-bottom left and 31 (Photodisc), 32 (John Humble / Photographer's Choice); Jim Merli / Visuals Unlimited: 5-middle and 22, 11, 21, 29; Visual and Written SL / Kike Calvo / Alamy Images: 13, 15.

ro/o6

Library of Congress Cataloging-in-Publication Data

Lockwood, Sophie.
  Gila monsters / by Sophie Lockwood.
    p. cm. — (The world of reptiles)
  Includes bibliographical references (p.   ) and index.
  ISBN 1-59296-547-4 (library bound : alk. paper)
  1. Gila monster—Juvenile literature. I. Title.
  QL666.L247L63 2006
  597.95'952—dc22   2005024789

TABLE OF CONTENTS

Chapter One

In the Sonoran Desert

The sun rises over the Sonoran Desert. It is spring, the time when Gila monsters emerge from their winter slumber. Gila monsters are most active in the spring. It is when their favorite foods are available and when they mate. The rest of the year, Gila monsters prefer to stay in underground burrows or in sheltered rock caves.

Rain has brought the desert to life. Poppies and brittlebush sprinkle yellow across the desert floor. Organ-pipe cacti stretch their thin limbs skyward. Ironwood and paloverde trees provide welcome shade against the growing warmth of the sun.

A desert spiny lizard perches near a puddle. It picks off insects as they come to drink. Nearby, a desert tortoise munches on the leaves of a wolfberry bush. A feisty roadrunner duels with a small rattlesnake. Surprisingly, the crafty roadrunner wins and is rewarded with a meal.

Gila Monster Fast Facts
(Heloderma suspectum)
Adult length: 20 to 21 inches (50 to 53 centimeters)
Weight: 3 to 5 pounds (1.4 to 2.3 kilograms)
Coloration: Black head and tongue; body has black markings mixed with yellow, orange, or pink
Range: Southwestern United States and the desert regions of northwest Mexico
Reproduction: 3 to 13 eggs per clutch
Diet: Eggs, young rodents, small mammals, small reptiles, **carrion**

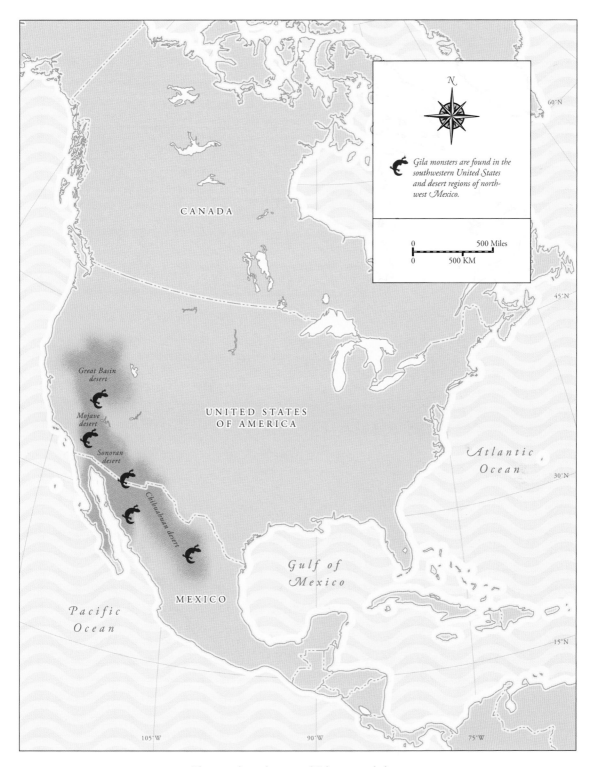

CANADA

N

Gila monsters are found in the
southwestern United States
and desert regions of northwest Mexico.

0		500 Miles
0		500 KM

60°N

45°N

Great Basin
desert

Mojave
desert

Sonoran
desert

Chihuahuan desert

UNITED STATES
OF AMERICA

Atlantic
Ocean

30°N

Gulf of
Mexico

MEXICO

Pacific
Ocean

15°N

105°W

90°W

75°W

This map shows the range of Gila monster habitats.

A Gila monster in the Sonoran Desert blends into its surroundings. The Sonoran Desert covers 120,000 square miles (310,800 square kilometers) in southeastern California, southwestern Arizona, much of the Mexican state of Baja California, and the western portion of the Mexican state of Sonora.

The Gila monster is hungry. He has not eaten for months. Fasting is not dangerous for Gila monsters. Their bodies are well-adapted to desert life. Scientists believe that an adult Gila monster can survive by eating just three or four large meals a year.

The Gila monster flicks his tongue to taste the air. Many scents blow on the wind, but he picks out his favorite: Gambel's quail. It has been a boom year for the quail. Wet winter weather has the desert blooming with fresh, green plants. Quail eat seeds, berries, and other plant matter. Female quails build their nests on the ground. They scrape a bowl shape into the ground, line it with grass, and deposit about a dozen off-white eggs. For a Gila monster, quail eggs are a king's feast.

The Gila monster moves slowly toward the quail's nest. Slow is the standard speed for Gila monsters. He flicks his tongue regularly to make sure he is moving in the right direction. He crawls to the nest and begins feeding.

Although Gila monsters usually eat their prey whole, they rarely do so with eggs. Our male cracks open his first egg and laps the egg's contents with his tongue. The rich yolk provides needed protein. The lizard takes his time. A feast like this

Did You Know?
Gila monsters are the largest lizards in the United States. Of the more than 4,500 lizard species in the world, only the Gila monsters and Mexican beaded lizards are venomous.

should not be gulped down in a minute. An hour passes before the Gila monster finishes the last egg. He moves his black tongue around the outside of his mouth to get the very last drop.

The morning desert is a busy place. Rattlesnakes and chuckwallas find comfortable rocks on which to sun their bodies. Coyotes curl up beneath leafy acacia trees for naps. A red-tailed hawk swoops down and grabs its breakfast—a young gopher snake. The Gila monster has had enough of the surface world. It is time to return to the burrow.

The Gila monster settles down for a nap. His burrow is comfortable and roomy. It has the added advantage of having been built by another animal—the desert tortoise. Many animals take advantage of the tunneling skills of desert tortoises. Empty tortoise burrows are in high demand. The Gila monster will defend his space against any visitors looking for lodging. He may be slow and sluggish, but he has a surprise waiting for daring intruders. His bite carries venom—enough to kill most animals foolish enough to get too close.

A Gila monster emerges from its burrow. It has been estimated that a Gila monster spends about 95 percent of its life in or at the mouth of its burrow.

Chapter Two

Scales and Tails

Gila monsters are members of the order Squamata. They are lizards, and their closest relatives are Mexican beaded lizards. Gila monsters and Mexican beaded lizards belong to a small family called Helodermatidae. *Helo* means "studded" or "warty," and *derma* means "skin." Scientists believe that their warty skin is much like the skin that protected some dinosaurs millions of years ago.

Although Gila monsters and beaded lizards look alike, they do have differences. Gila monsters tend to be shorter and wider and weigh less. They like sandy or gravel-covered desert with scruffy thorn or sage bushes. Beaded lizards prefer dry, open forests where there are plenty of rocks for hiding, and they live farther south than Gila monsters. Beaded lizards usually mate in the spring when the weather is not too hot. Gila monsters usually mate in late spring or early summer. These differences are small and depend mostly on the environment in which each type of lizard is found. The two cousins have many more similarities that bond them together: bony scales, unusual tails, and venomous bites.

Mexican beaded lizards have short, powerful legs.

A female Gila monster pops her head out of her burrow. She lives in a shallow cave under a cluster of large rocks. Although the ground is rough and the rocks sharp, she doesn't worry about bruises. She has skin like armor.

Gila monsters have evenly spaced, even-sized scales on their skin. Inside each scale or bead is a small bit of bone, called an osteoderm. These bony bits make the skin very tough. Gila monsters live in rugged habitats, and their skin helps protect them.

While the skin is hard, it is also somewhat **porous.** Gila monsters lose water through their skin, just like humans lose water by sweating. In the desert, this is dangerous. Loss of body water can mean death. While most lizards, snakes, and turtles bask in the hot sun, Gila monsters retreat into damp, cool dens. They spend about 95 percent of their time underground. They are among the few reptiles that prefer cool temperatures over warm ones.

Scientists think that Gila monster colors are warning signs. Gila monsters are black with bright yellow, orange, or pink markings. Bright colors in animals usually announce, "I've got poison here. Don't bother me."

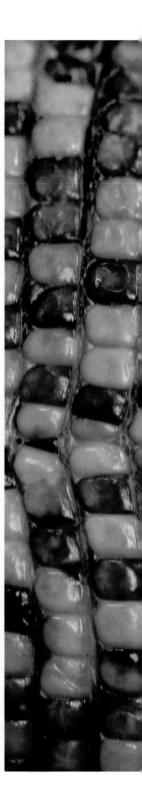

The skin of a Gila monster is made up of evenly spaced scales or beads. Each bead contains an osteoderm, a bony bit that makes the skin very tough and hard.

*The fat in this Gila monster's tail will help it
survive when food is scarce.*

TAILS

Many lizards use their tails for balance or defense against **predators.** A chameleon can wrap its tail around a branch like a "fifth limb." If anoles have their tails bitten off by predators, they can grow new ones. Gila monsters use their tails like kitchen pantries.

Gila monsters store fat in their tails. The lizards' bodies are shaped like sausages, and their tails are an extension of the sausage shape. As the lizards feed, their tails get chubbier. A well-fed Gila monster can have a remarkably plump tail.

A typical meal can equal about one-third of a lizard's body weight. The lizards' bodies use very little nutrition from each meal. Their **metabolism** is very slow. During lean times, the lizards' bodies convert tail fat into usable food energy.

TONGUES, TEETH, AND VENOM

Gila monsters have forked tongues, like snakes. They use their tongues for three senses: touch, taste, and smell. As the lizard comes out of its burrow, it tastes the air with its tongue. The scent of desert tortoise is in the air. That scent could lead to a nest where the

Did You Know?
A Gila monster's most sensitive organ is its tongue, which is slightly forked at the tip and 2 to 3 inches (5 to 7.5 centimeters) long. When the lizard is bothered, it shoots out its tongue and tastes the air. In addition to being the center for three senses, the tongue is also used to measure distance and express happiness.

Gila monster might find a meal of delicious eggs. The information gathered by the tongue helps the lizard determine how far away the nest is and how deep it is buried.

The scent of a predator is also in the wind, and the Gila monster tastes it. Coyote! The monster slips deeper into its burrow. The coyote begins to sniff around. The monster hisses a warning. Coyotes prey on Gila monsters, but they do so carefully.

The Gila monster's best protection is its venomous bite. They bite like bulldogs. Their jaws are extremely powerful. They bite down and hold on with clenched jaws. Their teeth are sharp and grooved along the bottom. It is the bite that delivers venom into their victims.

Gila monsters have a very strange method of injecting venom. The venom **glands** lie in the lower jaw. The lizards do not have hollow fangs like snakes. Once they bite down, venom pours into their mouths and mixes with saliva. Although they swallow their own venom, Gila monsters do not get poisoned. Other animals are not so lucky.

The lizards inject venom with repeated bites. Each bite breaks the victim's skin, and the venom flows in with the saliva. For most animals, death comes in twenty seconds to seven minutes.

Did You Know?
Bites from Gila monsters rarely kill humans. The lizards cannot deliver enough venom. The bites, however, are very painful and bring on swollen skin, vomiting, and fainting.

Gila monsters use their tongues to detect the presence of food and predators.

Chapter Three

An Underground Life

Early summer comes to the Sonoran Desert. It is time for Gila monsters to mate. The female may look ugly to humans, but she is beautiful to a male Gila monster. She is three years old, and this is the first year she can breed. Her body gives off a scent that attracts male Gila monsters.

Two large males taste the female's scent on the air. They both are interested in this young, nubby beauty, but only one will get to mate with her.

The males face off in a wrestling match that boggles the mind. They snort and bob their heads. They hiss and press their heads together. Bodies twist and writhe. This wrestling match isn't over in three falls. It may go on for hours.

In the end, the stronger male wins. The winner gets the female. The loser limps away for a much-needed rest.

REPRODUCTION

Females dig shallow nests for their eggs. The nests are about 5 inches (12.5 cm) deep and usually in a sandy area. The female Gila monster deposits from six to thir-

teen eggs. In this case, the number is only seven. Younger, smaller females lay fewer eggs than older, larger females. The young mother buries the eggs under sand and stones. Her work is done. It is time to retreat to the burrow.

The eggs develop over five to seven months or longer. The amount of time from laying to hatching depends on the weather conditions. When baby Gila monsters are ready to hatch, they struggle to get out of their shells. The **hatchlings** eat the remaining egg yolk. The newborns look

Gila monster eggs are oval in shape and have a shell that feels like leather.

A baby Gila monster emerges from its egg.

just like their parents, only smaller. They measure about 6 inches (15 cm) long and weigh about 1 ounce (28 grams). They come equipped with poison, so even a baby can inflict a serious bite.

The hatchlings grow quickly at first. Over time, their growth rate slows. Adult Gila monsters may grow only a fraction of an inch each year. Well-fed adults may grow slightly faster than those living where food is scarce.

A LIZARD'S LIFE

Gila monster hatchlings must find their own food, shelter, and water. They are fully prepared to survive. They've got active venom glands and the **instinct** to bite and deliver their poison.

The first order of business is finding a burrow. They can dig their own burrows, but are happy to take over a nice home left by some other animal. For a small lizard, a shallow space under a convenient rock makes a fine temporary burrow.

Gila monsters usually have two burrows. The winter burrow is deeper and safer, just right for **hibernating.** The summer burrow is shallower, just right for **estivating.** These lizards snooze through winter *and* summer sleep periods.

Finding food in the spring is easy. Gila monsters love fresh eggs. They'll follow the scent of Gambel's quail, roadrunners, or other reptiles to their nests. They crack the eggs and lap the innards with their forked tongues. While eggs are their favorite foods, Gila monsters also eat baby rabbits, baby mice or rats, other small mammals, lizards, and insects. They usually hunt on the ground but have been known to climb trees to get at nests.

Gila monsters face many predators. Coyotes, hawks, and owls are dangerous predators because Gila monsters are very slow moving. Their skin, with its bright-colored splotches, provides good **camouflage** in the dim light of dawn when the lizards are most active. They also hiss to chase away predators. When all else fails, there's always the poisonous bite. But predators will win out over most hatchlings. The most destructive predators are humans. Unfortunately, that's true for many wild animals.

If all goes well, a Gila monster may live about twenty years. Of course, 95 percent of those years will be spent sleeping, resting, or just hanging around the burrow. For monsters, it's almost always naptime.

A Gila monster raids a bird's nest for eggs.

One Man's Opinion
"I think a man who is fool enough to get bitten by a Gila Monster ought to die. The creature is so sluggish and slow of movement that the victim of its bite is compelled to help largely in order to get bitten."

Dr. Ward, *Arizona Graphic*, September 23, 1899

Chapter Four

Legends and Lore

The Gila monster has been the source of plenty of interesting myths, legends, and lies. Fear causes people to exaggerate the threat of these lizards. The tales may be false, but the fear is very real. For instance, a rock on an old Indian trail west of Phoenix bears a picture of two Gila monsters chasing a man running for his life. The truth is that Gila monsters are slow moving and would rather hide than chase.

For many years, Apaches panicked over any contact with Gila monsters. It was said that many elderly Apaches feared the lizards and no amount of money would convince them to go near a Gila monster.

Many people of Mexico believed that Gila monsters breathed death. It was said that one puff of lizard breath in the face would cause a victim to die. This is another exaggeration, but that doesn't mean that lizard breath isn't revolting. In 1890, *Scientific American* reported that a Gila monster "emits its breath in a series of quick gasps. The breath is very fetid [foul] and its odor can be

detected at some little distance from the lizard." Yet, no one ever died from inhaling bad breath.

One strange myth claims that once a Gila monster bites down, it won't let go until sunset or a thunderstorm arrives. These animals do have a strong bite, and they don't let go easily. No one, however, has ever observed an event like the one described in this story.

An even stranger idea was that Gila monsters have no **anal** opening. People actually believed that the lizards took in food but did not pass solid waste out of their bodies. This, they claimed, explained the horrid bad breath in Gila monsters. These animals do pass **feces,**

but because they take in only small amounts of food, and use that food well, they produce very little solid waste. In reality, the bad breath is probably caused by a buildup of gases in the lizards' stomachs. They digest their meals so slowly that the food has a chance to rot before it is fully processed by the body.

MEDICAL VALUE

Gila monsters have very little value for humans, except when it comes to medicine. Many years ago, doctors and tribal healers tried using Gila monster venom to treat Parkinson's disease. This disease attacks the human nervous system, and patients lose control of their muscles. Gila monster venom paralyzes the nervous system of small mammals and birds. It was believed that watered-down venom might help control the shaking and seizures caused by Parkinson's.

In 2001, scientists performed experiments on rats using Gila monster venom. The scientists discovered that small doses of the venom increased memory in rats. There is hope that further study might lead to a treatment for Alzheimer's disease, a condition that affects memory, usually in older people.

More promising is a potential cure for type 2 diabetes. People who have diabetes don't produce the right amount of insulin in their bodies. Insulin is a substance that helps the body use sugars and starches. Gila monsters naturally produce a substance known as exendin-4. Some studies have shown that this substance encourages the body to produce its own insulin. If treatments using exendin-4 work, it will be a remarkable advance for diabetes sufferers. Just think—a medicine that could help millions of people might come from a family of venomous lizards!

The Gila monster's venom glands are located in its mouth.

Chapter Five

Man and Monsters

A family has a home built in the suburbs outside of Tucson, Arizona. In September, the builders level the ground and dig a foundation. They pour cement, hammer nails, and drive their trucks over the land. In February, the family moves into their new home with its fenced-in yard. They have no idea that their fence surrounds the winter home of a Gila monster.

Spring comes and the Gila monster ends its winter sleep, only to find a jungle gym and some scruffy grass where she used to hunt. The kids come out to play. They find a brightly colored animal digging in the sandbox—a very dangerous critter. The Gila monster would not choose to attack a human, but curious kids often put themselves in danger's path. Not surprisingly, police and fire departments throughout Arizona get many "Gila monster calls" every year.

THREATS TO SURVIVAL

Natural threats to Gila monsters are many. They live underground, so floods in their home territories are deadly. A

When subdivisions such as this one outside Tucson, Arizona, are built, many Gila monsters lose their natural habitat.

serious hot spell, bitter winter cold, or forest fire are all threats to survival. Predators eat some lizards, particularly the **juveniles.** None of these events, however, causes the destruction associated with humans.

For some reason, humans have decided that venomous lizards make good pets. They are not dogs or cats. They don't do tricks. They can't even be held or cuddled, so what is the attraction? Some people just have to have an exotic pet, whether that pet will fare well in their care or not. It is against the law in areas where Gila monsters live to capture, bother, or kill one. Yet, humans continue to capture Gila monsters for the pet trade.

As people spread into the desert, there simply isn't enough room left for the creatures that normally live there. Gila monsters lose habitat to homes, golf courses, parks, and highways. The loss of habitat is the most serious threat to Gila monster existence.

Agriculture results in more habitat loss. Water is rerouted into former desert. Tomatoes, lettuce, and melons replace thorn scrub and cactus. Farming changes the land dramatically. Rocks—good burrowing locations—are removed. Watering keeps the ground too wet for a comfortable underground burrow. Ground-nesting birds and reptiles no longer nest in farmland. Gila monsters in farm territory lose their homes and their food supply.

Building highways through the desert is one human activity
that threatens the survival of Gila monsters.

33

Cotton is harvested on a farm in Arizona. Irrigation makes farming possible on dry desert land.

In addition, farming brings chemical changes to the soil. Farmers spread fertilizer on the soil to make plants grow. They spray chemicals to kill bugs and other pests. Those chemicals **pollute** the soil. When rains come, the runoff water carries the chemicals to wilderness areas, and pollution spreads. Wildlife, including Gila monsters, in and near farm districts suffers from this pollution.

HELP ON THE WAY

Help is on the way to protect Gila monsters. Laws protect them from hunters and collectors. These laws are hard to enforce, but may discourage a person who sees one of these lizards in the wild from taking it home.

Scientists are studying Gila monsters to find out more about their lifestyle and what they need for survival. This is not an easy task. When an animal spends 95 percent

Biologists and other scientists are working to find out more about Gila monsters and how to help them survive.

of its life underground and few are seen, studying the species becomes difficult. Still, some scientists persist. They try to trap lizards in known feeding areas. They do not intend to harm the Gila monsters. They just want to put radio transmitters on the animals to track their daily lives. The knowledge the scientists gain may help the lizards to survive.

Conservation groups help by educating the public. They have a hard job. It is easy to convince people to save dolphins or tigers or koalas. Reptiles are not as popular. Still, nature depends on a balance among all species of animals.

All creatures play a role in Mother Nature's drama. Small animals eat seeds and insects. Larger animals eat smaller ones. Gila monsters help control growing populations of rabbits and other animals. Without these lizard species, nature's balance may get a bit wobbly. When too many rabbits live in an area, they may go from being sweet little bunnies to serious pests. So even the homely Gila monster plays a part in keeping the delicate balance of nature. In the web of life, we are all connected.

Glossary

anal (A-nul) referring to the anus, an opening through which solid waste is emptied from an animal's body

camouflage (KAM-uh-flahzh) natural coloring that allows an animal or plant to blend in with its surroundings

carrion (KAR-ee-un) the flesh of a dead animal

conservation (con-sur-VAY-shuhn) the act of saving or preserving some aspect of wildlife

estivating (ESS-ti-vate-ing) the act of sleeping for long periods during summer months

feces (FEE-seez) solid waste of an animal

glands (GLANDS) organs that produce a chemical substance or let other substances leave the body

hatchlings (HACH-lingz) newborns that have just emerged from their eggs

hibernating (HYE-bur-nate-ing) sleeping for a long period through the winter

instinct (IN-stingkt) one's natural sense of what is happening with one's body, or actions one takes

juveniles (JOO-vuh-nuhlz) youngsters, like human toddlers

metabolism (muh-TAB-uh-liz-uhm) the bodily process of turning food into energy

pollute (puh-LOOT) fouling of air, water, or land by waste, chemicals, or other contaminating agents

porous (POR-uhss) having holes or pores that liquids can seep through

predators (PRED-uh-turz) animals that hunt and kill other animals for food

For More Information

Watch It

World's Last Great Places: Sonoran Desert, A Violent Eden. VHS (Washington, D.C., National Geographic, 1997).

Read It

Arnosky, Jim. *All About Reptiles.* New York: Scholastic, 2004.

Miller, Jake. *The Gila Monster.* New York: PowerKids Press, 2003.

Pratt-Serafini, Kristin Joy. *Saguaro Moon: A Desert Journal.* Nevada City, Calif.: Dawn Publications, 2002.

Look It Up

Visit our home page for lots of links about Gila monsters: *http://www.childsworld.com/links*

Note to Parents, Teachers, and Librarians: We routinely verify our Web links to make sure they are safe, active sites—so encourage your readers to check them out!

The Animal Kingdom
Where Do Gila Monsters Fit In?

Kingdom: Animal

Phylum: Chordata

Class: Reptilia

Order: Squamata

Family: Helodermatidae

Genus: *Heloderma*

Species: *suspectum*

Index

About the Author

Sophie Lockwood is a former teacher and a longtime writer. She writes textbooks, newspaper articles, and magazine articles. Sophie enjoys writing about animals and their habits. The most interesting part of her research, Sophie says, is learning how scientists apply their knowledge to save endangered species. She lives with her husband in the foothills of the Blue Ridge Mountains.